Bug Bab

70101257

Catherine Veitch

Heinemann
LIBRARY
Chicago, Illinois

© 2013 Heinemann Library
an imprint of Capstone Global Library, LLC
Chicago, Illinois

To contact Capstone Global Library please phone 800-747-4992, or visit our website www.capstonepub.com

All rights reserved. No part of this publication may be reproduced or transmitted in any form or by any means, electronic or mechanical, including photocopying, recording, taping, or any information storage and retrieval system, without permission in writing from the publisher.

Edited by Daniel Nunn, Rebecca Rissman, and Catherine Veitch
Designed by Cynthia Della-Rovere
Picture research by Ruth Blair
Production by Victoria Fitzgerald
Originated by Capstone Global Library

Library of Congress Cataloging-in-Publication Data
Veitch, Catherine.
Bug babies / Catherine Veitch.
pages cm.—(Animal babies)
Includes bibliographical references and index.
ISBN 978-1-4329-7495-4 (hb)
ISBN 978-1-4329-8420-5 (pb)
1. Arthropoda—Infancy—Juvenile literature. 2. Worms—Infancy—Juvenile literature. I. Title.
QL434.15.V45 2013
595.1392—dc23 2012033409

Acknowledgments
Dreamstime: Halil I. Inci, 21; Getty Images: Dorling Kindersley, 6, Heidi & Hans-Juergen Koch/Minden Pictures, 9, Mark Moffett/Minden Pictures, 14; Nature Picture Library: Kim Taylor, 10, Martin Dohrn, 8, Meul/ARCO, 16, 18, Paul Harcourt Davies, 1, 13 Right, 23 Middle, Simon Colmer, 22 Top; Shutterstock: Cathy Keifer, 2, 11 Left, 23 Top, D. Kucharski K. Kucharska, 5 Bottom Right, Dr Morley Read, 19, FloridaStock, 5 Left, 23 Bottom, Gherasim Rares, 15, irin-k, 5 Top Right, James Laurie, 11 Right, Kletr, 20, kurt_G, Cover, 17, PHOTO FUN, Back Cover, 7, Sim Kay Seng, 4, Subbotina Anna, 22 Left, Sue Robinson, 12, Torsten Dietrich, 13 Left, vaklav, 22 Right

We would like to thank Michael Bright for his invaluable help in the preparation of this book.

Every effort has been made to contact copyright holders of material reproduced in this book. Any omissions will be rectified in subsequent printings if notice is given to the publisher.

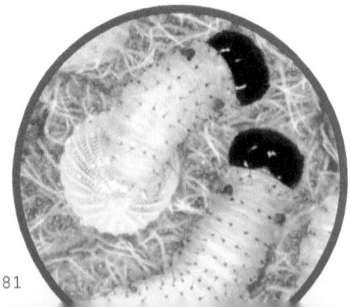

Printed in the United States 5581

Contents

What Is a Bug? 4
How Are Baby Bugs Born? 6
Caring for Baby Bugs 14
Growing Up 18
Life Cycle of a Bug 22
Picture Glossary 23
Index 24
Notes to Parents and Teachers . . 24

What Is a Bug?

A bug is a small animal.

Spiders are bugs.
Insects and worms are bugs.

How Are Baby Bugs Born?

Many bugs lay eggs.
Some bugs lay eggs on soil.

Some bugs lay eggs
on leaves.

Some bugs lay eggs on water.

Some bugs lay eggs on food.

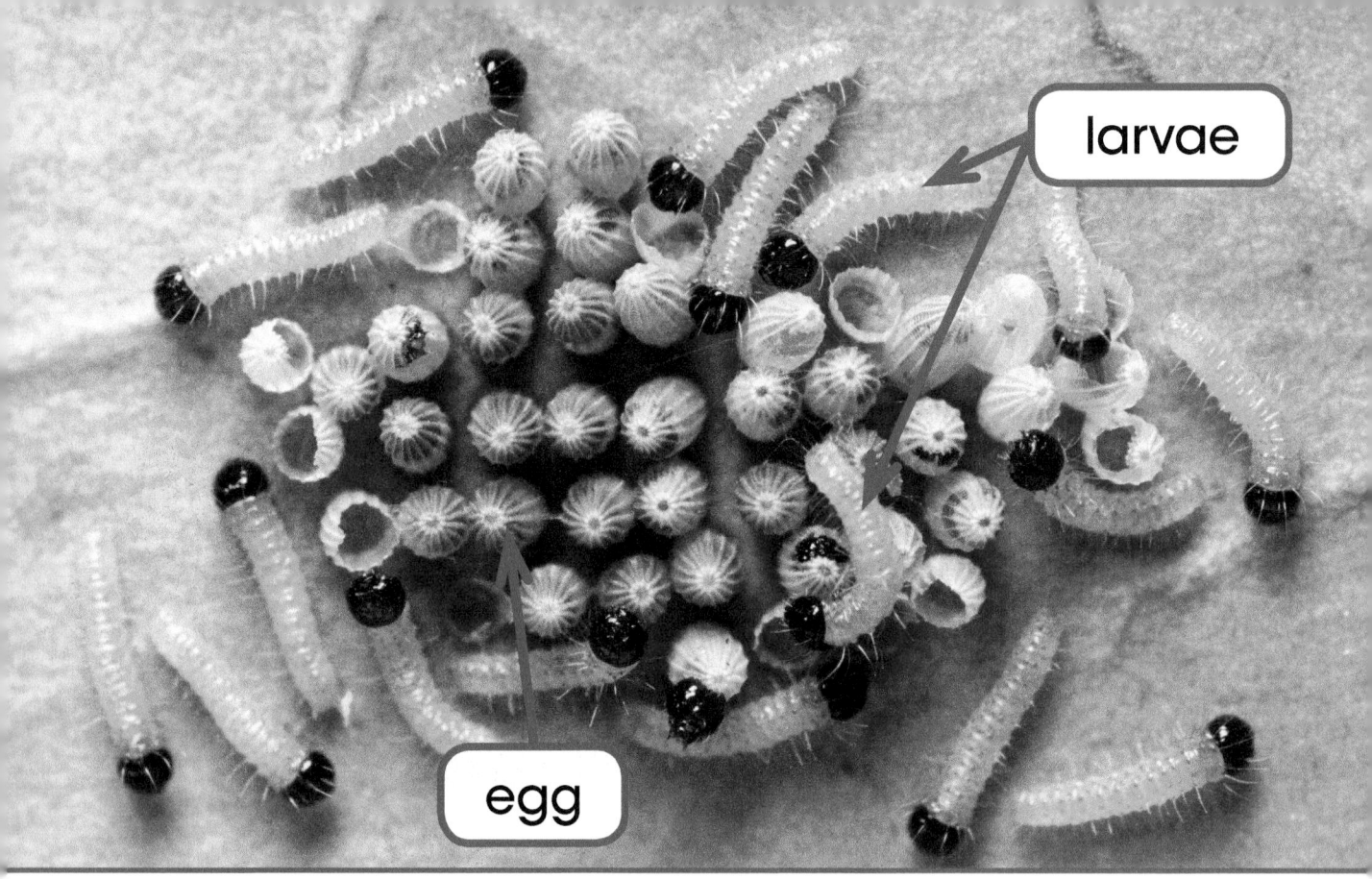

Larvae can hatch from eggs.

Larvae do not look like their parents.

Nymphs can hatch from eggs.

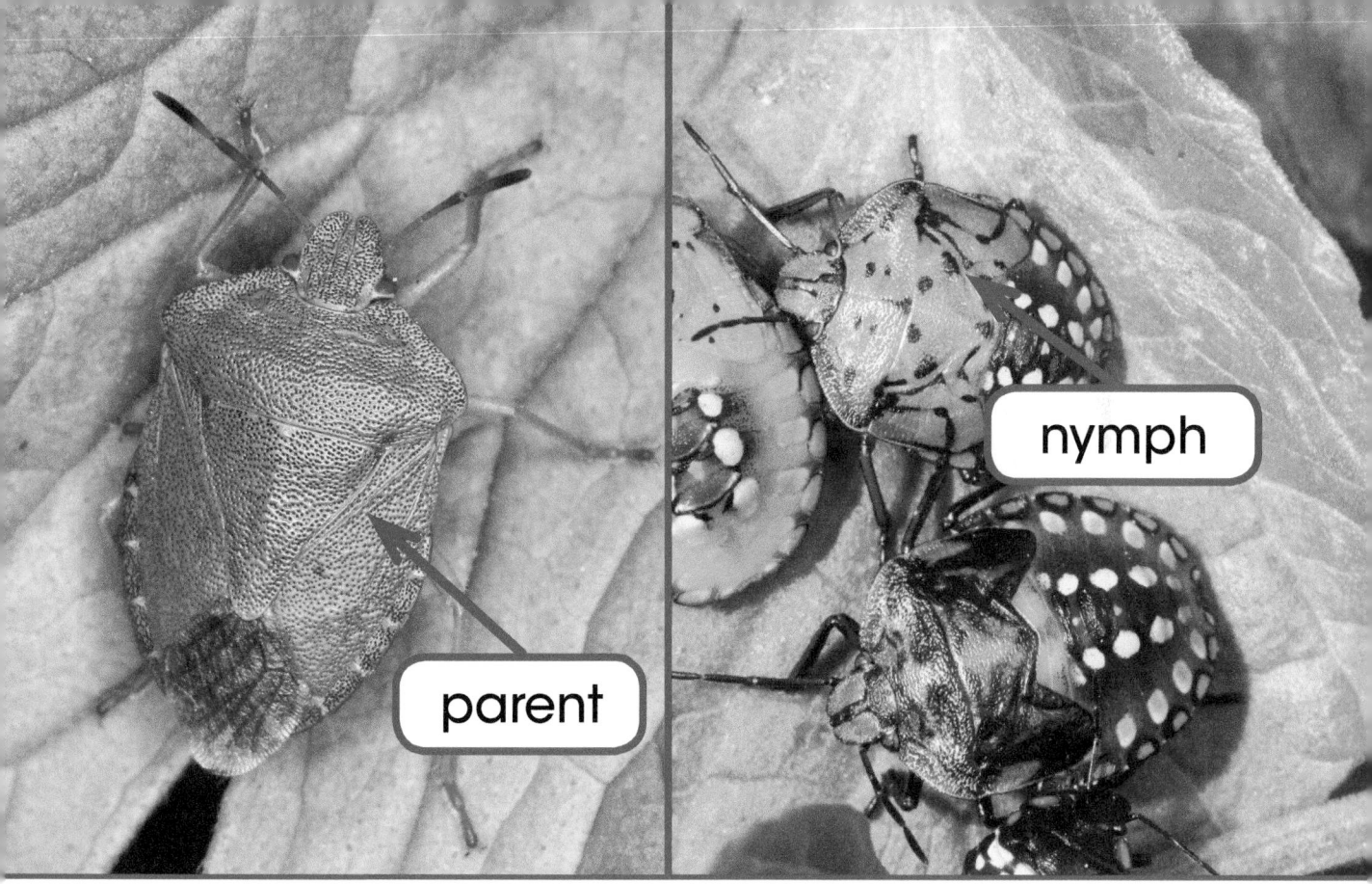

Nymphs look like their parents.

Caring for Baby Bugs

Some bugs care for their babies.

These worker bees bring food to their larvae.

This ant carries its baby to a safe place.

This spider carries its babies on its back.

Growing Up

Many bug babies care for themselves. Some feed on smaller bugs.

Some feed on plants.

Some bugs find a new home.

They hide from predators.

Life Cycle of a Bug

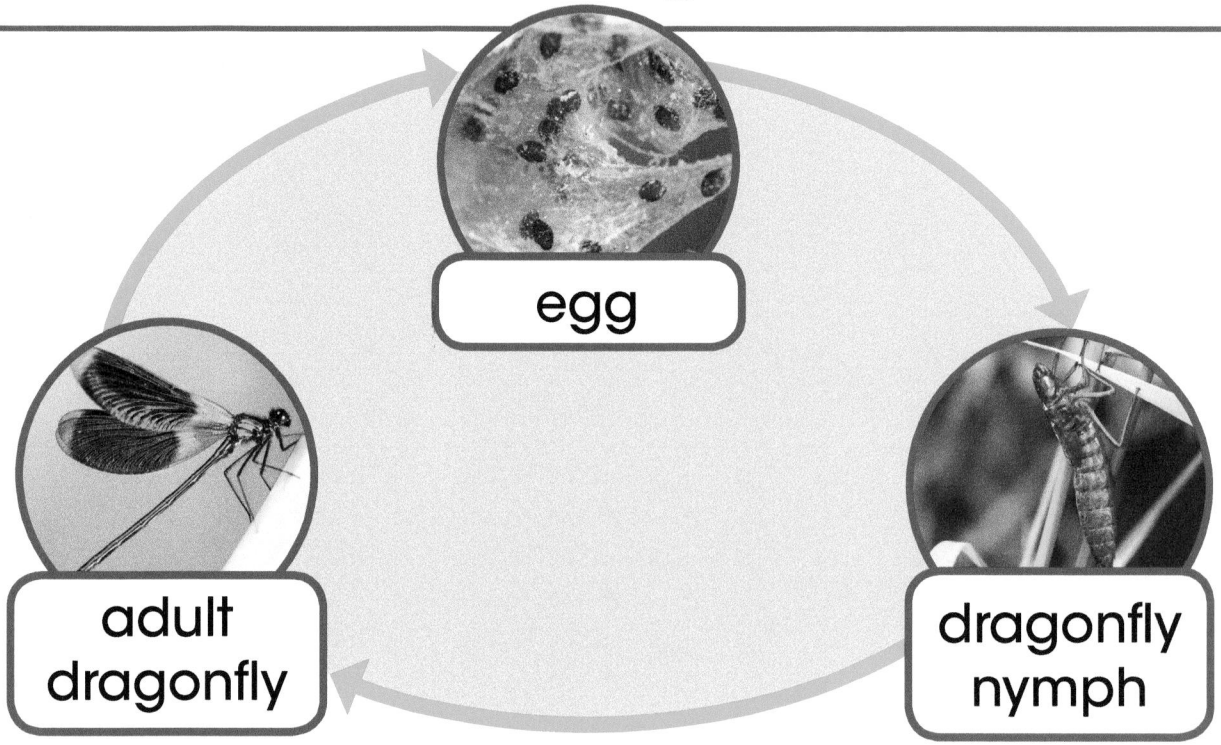

A life cycle shows the different stages of an animal's life. This is the life cycle of a dragonfly.

Picture Glossary

larva stage some bugs have when they first hatch. More than one is larvae.

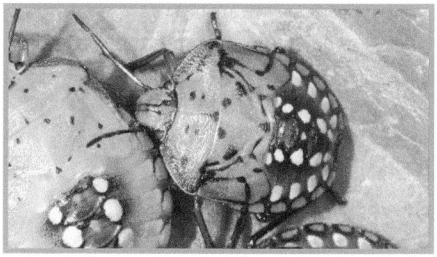

nymph stage some bugs have when they first hatch

predator animal that eats other animals

Index

bug babies 14, 17, 18
eggs 6, 7, 8, 9, 10, 12
food 15, 18, 19
larvae 10, 11, 15, 23
nymphs 12, 13, 23
predators 21, 23

Notes to Parents and Teachers

Before reading

Show children a collection of photos and videos of bugs. National Geographic and PBS are useful websites. Explain what a bug is and discuss the characteristics of bugs.

After reading

- Mount photos of adult and baby bugs on note cards and play games of concentration where the children have to match a baby bug with its parent. Model the correct pairs first.
- Ask children to label the parts of a bug: for example, wings, head, legs, antennae.
- Look at page 22 and discuss the life cycle stages of a bug. Mount photos of the egg, nymph, and adult stages and ask children to put the photos in order. Encourage children to draw a life cycle of a human to compare. Compare how different bugs care for their babies. Discuss the care human babies need.
- Some children will be curious to learn the names of the bugs. Therefore, to extend children's knowledge, the bugs are as follows: dragonfly: p. 4; spider, ladybug, worm: p. 5; snail eggs: p. 6; butterfly eggs: p. 7; mosquito eggs: p. 8; house fly: p. 9; cabbage white butterfly larvae and eggs: p. 10; monarch butterfly larvae and eggs, monarch butterfly: p. 11; green shield bug nymphs: p. 12; green shield bug parent and nymphs: p. 13; earwig: p. 14; worker bees and larvae: p. 15; yellow mound ant with pupa: p. 16; wolf spider and spiderlings: p. 17; ladybug larvae: p. 18; caterpillar: p. 19; wasp spiderlings: p. 20; caterpillar: p. 21.